INCREDIBLY CURIOUS Questions and Answers

INCREDIBLY

CURIOUS

Questions and Answers

Words by Camilla de la Bédoyère and Anne Rooney

Illustrations by Genie Espinosa (cover), Pauline Reeves, Leire Martín, Ana Gomez and Richard Watson

MILES KELLY

First published in 2019 by Miles Kelly Publishing Ltd
Harding's Barn, Bardfield End Green, Thaxted, Essex, CM6 3PX, UK

Copyright © Miles Kelly Publishing Ltd 2019

2 4 6 8 10 9 7 5 3 1

Publishing Director Belinda Gallagher
Creative Director Jo Cowan
Editorial Director Rosie Neave
Senior Editor Amy Johnson
Designers Rob Hale, Joe Jones, Simon Lee
Image Manager Liberty Newton
Production Elizabeth Collins, Jennifer Brunwin-Jones
Reprographics Stephan Davis, Callum Ratcliffe-Bingham
Assets Lorraine King

ISBN 978-1-78617-835-0

Printed in China

British Library Cataloguing-in-Publication Data
A catalogue record for this book is available from the British Library

Made with paper from a sustainable forest

www.mileskelly.net

CONTENTS

Animals

What is an animal?

Animals are living things that do all of these things...

① Have babies

All animals can make new life like themselves – this is called **having babies**, or **reproduction**.

② Breathe

Animals **breathe** to take air into their bodies. The body needs a gas in the air called oxygen to keep working.

③ Use senses

An animal uses the **senses** of touch, taste, smell, sight and hearing to find out what is going on around it.

Those leaves look tasty!

④ Move

Most animals **move** to get to food and water, to find safe places, and to escape from danger.

> I learnt to stand up 30 minutes after I was born. How old were you when you learnt to stand?

⑤ Eat

Animals must **eat** food to stay alive. Food gives them energy so they can **move** and **grow**.

Munch!

⑥ Get rid of waste

Waste is leftover food that an animal's body doesn't need.

> Waste not want not! Dung beetles like me use elephant poo for lots of things!

⑦ Grow

All animals start small and **grow** bigger until they are old enough to **have babies** of their own.

Why do crocodiles eat stones?

Because they swallow their meaty meals whole, and the stones help to grind up the food in their tummies!

Crocs are one of the world's biggest carnivores, or meat-eaters. We eat fish, birds, rats, snakes, lizards and even deer and pigs.

What makes flamingos pink?

Flamingos are pink because they eat pink shrimps that live in VERY salty lakes! They feed with their heads upside down.

Can you see any other upside-down eaters around here?

Who likes eating greens?

Leaves and other greens taste great to herbivores (plant-eaters) like sloths. Some greens are tough to eat, so they spend lots of time chewing.

Anteaters like me eat ants and termites — thousands of them every day! We lick them up with our long, sticky tongues.

Are animals picky eaters?

They can be! Some only eat one special food. Others, like tiger sharks and brown bears, will eat almost anything they can find!

What are senses?

Senses are the body's way of finding out about the world. Animals use senses to locate food, find their way about, avoid danger and make friends. The five main senses are **hearing**, **sight**, **smell**, **taste** and **touch**.

HEARING

Ear

Do bugs have ears?

Yes — lots of bugs can hear better than humans, but our ears can be in strange places! I'm a bush cricket, and my ears are on my legs.

TOUCH

What are whiskers for?

A cat's whiskers are super-sensitive. I use them to feel things — they can tell me if a space I want to crawl into is too small for my body.

How do snakes smell?

Snakes can smell with their tongues.
They flick them in the air to detect
any appealing pongs!

SMELL

TASTE

Why is it a bad idea to lick a frog?

I make a foul-tasting slime in my skin. It stops animals from eating me.

SIGHT

Do all animals have two eyes?

Some animals have more than two!
Most spiders have eight eyes but cave
spiders have none. They live in caves
where it's always dark.

Did you know?

A **fulmar** is a foul seabird. It spits a stinky oil at anyone who gets too close.

The **giraffe** is the tallest animal that lives on land.

Lobsters have blue blood and some dogs have blue tongues.

When a **sandtiger shark** wants to sink to the sea bed, it has to burp first!

A spiny **sea urchin** is covered in tiny feet. Its mouth is on its bottom!

Mimic octopuses can change shape and colour. They can pretend to be fish or sea snakes.

Sweat bees like the smell and taste of human sweat!

If a **sponge** is broken into bits, this strange sea creature is able to put itself back together again.

The **dung beetle** is the strongest animal on Earth. If it were the size of a human it could pull six buses full of people!

A **spider** eats about 2000 bugs a year.

Australian **burrowing frogs** cover themselves in slime, so when flies land on them they get stuck – and the frogs can gobble them up.

Bees waggle their bottoms in a crazy dance to tell each other where to find the best flowers.

Hippos don't just yawn when they are tired – they also yawn when they are angry or scared.

A **blue whale** eats millions of pink shrimps, so its poo is pink too. Each poo can be bigger than you!

A **catfish** can use its whole body to taste. Its skin is covered with taste buds.

What's inside an animal?

If you had to build an animal from scratch, here's what you would need...

Spine

① Framework

Most big animals have a **skeleton** – a framework of bones beneath their skin. Smaller animals have a tough outside – like a shell or strong skin – called an **exoskeleton**.

Ribs

③ Inner workings

Soft, squishy body parts called organs do useful jobs such as thinking, breathing and turning food into energy.

Brain

Tail

Lung

Liver

Heart

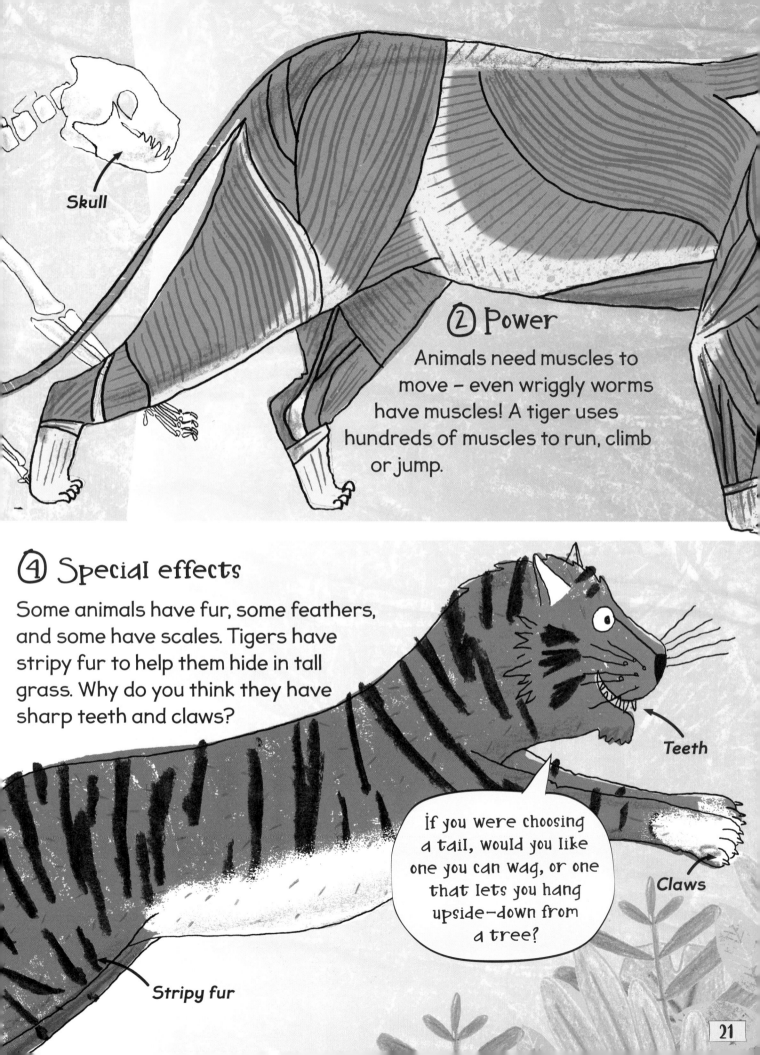

Skull

② Power

Animals need muscles to move – even wriggly worms have muscles! A tiger uses hundreds of muscles to run, climb or jump.

④ Special effects

Some animals have fur, some feathers, and some have scales. Tigers have stripy fur to help them hide in tall grass. Why do you think they have sharp teeth and claws?

Teeth

If you were choosing a tail, would you like one you can wag, or one that lets you hang upside-down from a tree?

Claws

Stripy fur

Why are you blue?

Colours and patterns make an animal beautiful! They can also make an animal look scary, or help it to hide.

Blue morpho butterfly

Blue-ringed octopus

My colour is a sign of danger. When I'm scared, blue circles appear on my skin. They are a warning that I can kill any attackers with venom.

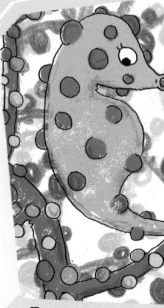

Danger or disguise?

Some animals blend into the background. This is called camouflage. Others have colours and patterns that warn enemies to stay away. Which of these creatures are using camouflage, and which are using warning colours?

Strawberry poison dart frog

Pygmy seahorse

Blue shark

My colours help me hide. A blue or dark grey shark can prowl through the sea, unseen by the fish it is looking for.

Would you rather have blue feet, like me, or a blue bum, like a baboon?

Blue-footed booby

Southern crowned-pigeon

My beautiful blue feathers make me look healthy and fit to attract a mate.

Leaf insect

Banded sea krait

Lion

Would you rather?

Winter is coming! Would you prefer to travel to somewhere warm, like a **sand martin**, or curl up and sleep through it, like a **dormouse**?

Zzzzz...

Would you rather be spotted like a **leopard**, or striped like a **tiger**?

Is it better to have a long neck, like a **giraffe**...

...or lots of arms like an **octopus**?

You look soooo cute!

A giraffe uses its long neck to reach leaves in tall trees. An octopus uses its arms to move, touch, taste and gather food.

If you were an animal baby would you prefer to sit in dad's pouch, like a **seahorse**, or in mum's, like a **kangaroo**?

It's picnic time! Would you prefer to tuck into a rotting dead animal like a **vulture**, or suck down some animal poo like a **sea cucumber**?

Erm... yummy?

Would you rather have armour like a **pangolin**, or spikes like a **pufferfish**?

WHOOSH!

Would you rather be able to dive through the air at 200 kilometres an hour like a **peregrine falcon**, or fly 15,000 kilometres in a single journey like an **albatross**?

Is it better to be best friends with a **shark** or a **crocodile**?

Sharks and crocodiles are both big carnivores. That means they eat other animals, so it's probably not a good idea to try to make friends with either!

Will you play with me?

Why do spiders do cartwheels?

TUMBLE

Desert spiders that have to get across hot sand do cartwheels so their feet don't get burnt!

How high can you jump?

BOUNCE

LEAP

Kangaroos can jump up to 3 metres into the air, but we can't walk, or move backwards.

Why do orang-utans have long arms?

Long arms are great for swinging through trees. We also have hands for gripping branches and grabbing fruit.

SWING

HOVER

Antelopes leap several metres at a time, springing up in the air to escape from danger.

Which bird flies, but goes nowhere?

A hummingbird does. It flaps and twists its wings so that it can hover in front of a flower, where it drinks the sweet nectar.

I can leap more than 100 times my own height.

SPRING

Fleas jump so they can leap from animal to animal, where they suck blood!

How fast do cheetahs sprint?

A cheetah is the fastest running animal on the planet. It can reach top speeds of up to 100 kilometres an hour.

① Built for speed

A cheetah's body is packed with small but powerful muscles.

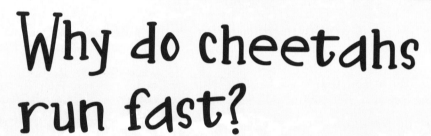

Why do cheetahs run fast?

Like many hunters, cheetahs turn on the speed when they want to catch their lunch! The antelope they chase need to be fast too, if they hope to escape.

Why are tortoises so slow?

Tortoises plod along slowly because they don't need speed to catch their lunch – they eat grass! They don't need to be fast to escape from danger either because their tough shells protect them like a suit of armour.

② Big strides

It has a super-bendy spine and long, slim legs.

③ Long leap

All four of a cheetah's feet leave the ground as it runs.

Why do crabs run sideways?

Because the way their legs bend means they can't run forwards!

Who's playing statues?

During the day, a potoo bird doesn't move at all! It pretends to be a branch. At night, it flies about, hunting bugs to eat.

How many?

An octopus has **3** hearts but an earthworm has **5**.

A squid has **2** tentacles...

... and it has **8** arms.

Sea otters have **800 million** hairs on their bodies.

Tree kangaroos can jump **30** metres from a tree to the ground below.

A snow leopard can leap more than **10** metres in a single bound.

A snake can live for up to **6** months without eating.

A giraffe's tongue is **45** centimetres long.

20 The number of hours three-toed sloths, koalas and lions might sleep in one day.

500,000

The number of kilometres a sooty tern can fly without stopping for a rest.

Monarch butterflies can go on incredible journeys – one butterfly flew more than **4000** kilometres to lay its eggs!

4

The number of wings a bee has.

1

The number of hours it takes a snail to slime its way along just **1** metre of ground.

The largest number of legs ever counted on a millipede. **750**

A mother cane toad can lay **35,000** eggs at a time.

36 The length, in centimetres, of the longest insect – a type of stick insect called Chan's megastick.

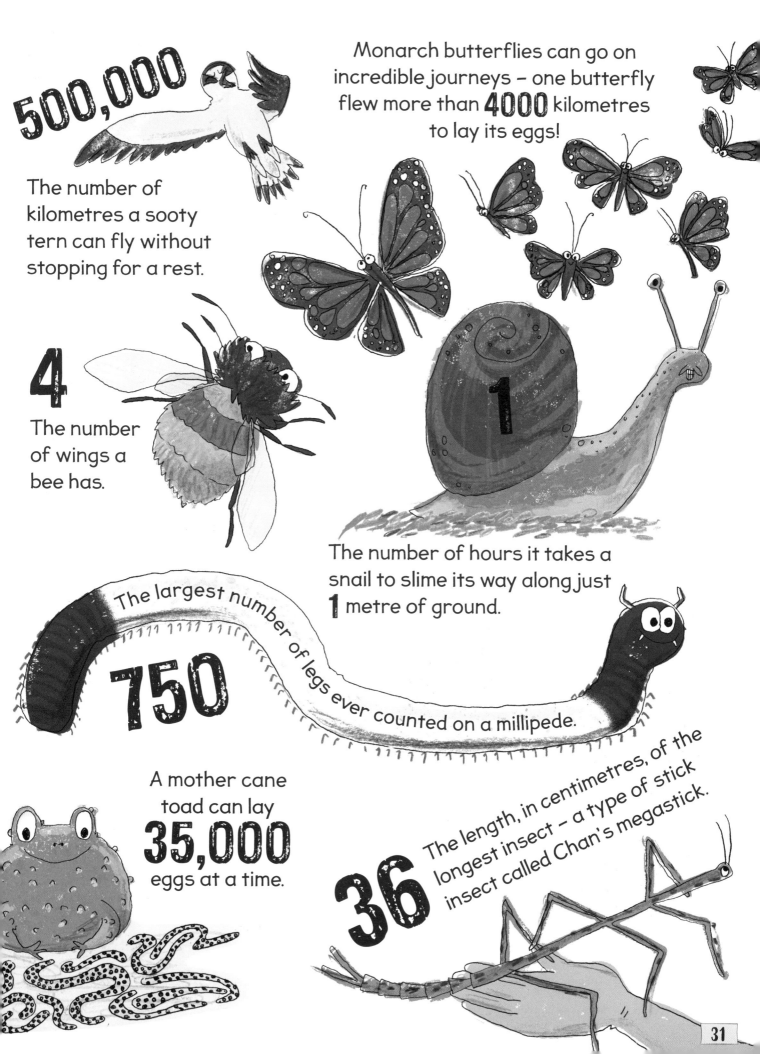

Is anyone at home?

Yes! An animal's home is a safe place where it can look after its babies. Animal homes are called habitats. They can be as big as an ocean or as small as a single leaf.

Froghopper nest

Who lives in a home made of spit?

Young froghopper insects build a home of froth around themselves! This 'spit' keeps them safe while they grow.

Why do frogs like water?

Because they need to lay their eggs in it. They are amphibians, which means they can live in water or on land.

Some animals that live in or near water have to come up to the surface to breathe air.

Others have gills and breathe underwater.

Frogs like to live in wet places

Birds nest in tree branches

Owls and their chicks live in tree holes

Why do owls hoot?

They hoot to tell other owls to stay away from their tree. Some animals don't like neighbours!

This fox den is under the tree's roots

Ladybirds also lay their eggs on leaves

Would you rather live in a treetop nest with chicks, or in an underground sett with badger cubs?

Can animals make things?

Yes, some animals are expert builders and can make super structures.

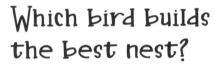

① *A hoop of grass...*

② *...turns into a ball...*

③ *...and then a home.*

Which bird builds the best nest?

A dad weaver bird makes his nest by stitching blades of grass together, then stuffing feathers inside to make a soft bed. He sings to tell mum she can lay her eggs there.

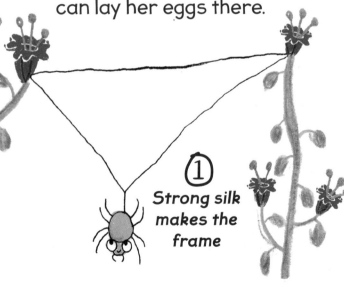

① *Strong silk makes the frame*

② *Sticky silk is used in the spiral*

Why do spiders build webs?

So they can trap flies. A spider makes the silk in its body and then spins it into a web.

Who loves mud?

Millions of termites do! They build their huge towering homes from mud. A group of termites that live together is called a colony, and their home can last for years.

There are passages, tunnels, and places to store food inside

A termite mound can be more than 2 metres high!

HOME SWEET HOME

A single queen lays all the eggs

What's the point of mums and dads?

Some animal babies look after themselves, but many need mums and dads to give them food and keep them safe.

Where do penguins keep their eggs?

Emperor penguins like us keep our eggs off the ice by holding them on our feet. The skin on our tummies is covered with fluffy feathers to keep our chicks warm.

How does a baby orca sleep?

Baby orcas can swim as soon as they are born, and they sleep while they are swimming! Orcas can rest one half of their brain at a time. The other half stays wide-awake.

A baby orca is called a calf

Do baby animals drink milk?

Yes, furry animals are called mammals and they feed their babies with milk. A polar bear mum looks after her cubs in a snowy den during the long, cold winter.

ZZZZZZ

Would you rather have an orca, a penguin or a polar bear for a parent?

A compendium of questions

Are sharks the most dangerous animals?

Sharks don't usually attack people. Snakes, donkeys and dogs hurt people more often than sharks!

I'm harmless to humans! I love to eat small fish, squid and jellyfish.

How does a squid escape from a hungry shark?

A squid squirts jets of water, and zooms off! The jets of water push the squid forward. This is called jet propulsion.

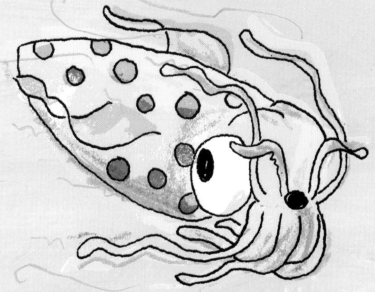

Can a lizard run across water?

A basilisk lizard can. It runs really fast and uses its big feet and tail to help it balance on top of the water.

Whip-like tail

Long toes

Why do jellyfish wobble?

Jellyfish don't have any bones and their bodies are full of water, like real jelly!

Do all animals have bones?

Mammals, birds, reptiles, amphibians and fish have bones. All other animals – including bugs, crabs and octopuses – don't.

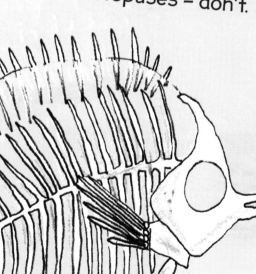

What is venom?

Venom is a poison. Venomous animals can inject it using their fangs, claws, spines or stings. They use it to defend themselves, or to kill animals for food.

Is a bat a bird?

No, it's a flying mammal. Bats are the only mammals that fly.

Do lions purr?

Big cats roar but can't purr, and small cats purr but can't roar. Big cats sometimes make a noise like a growly purr!

I'm safer from attack in the air than I would be running along the ground.

Do camels keep water in their humps?

No – a camel's hump is full of fat, not water.

The gliding lizard uses its long tail to steer through the air

How do animals glide?

Gliding lizards, frogs and squirrels have large flaps of skin that they stretch out before they leap from a tree. The skin works like a parachute to help them glide, and land softly.

What's the smallest bird?

A bee hummingbird. It's smaller than your thumb. An ostrich is the biggest bird.

How many animals are in the world?

No one knows, but there are billions of ants, so it must be lots!

Dinosaurs

When did dinosaurs live?

The first dinosaurs lived about 240 million years ago, long before there were people. Dinosaurs evolved from other animals called dinosauromorphs. They were cat-sized reptiles.

I'm a dinosauromorph. When an animal evolves it changes over time, so it can survive in a changing world.

I'm one of the first dinosaurs. I lived about 230 million years ago.

Herrerasaurus

Tarbosaurus

I'm one of the last dinosaurs. I roamed the planet 70 million years ago.

Were all dinosaurs huge?

Dinosaurs came in all shapes and sizes. The largest ones were called titanosaurs. They were more than 20 metres long and weighed as much as six elephants!

I'm one of the biggest dinosaurs ever. Can you guess where in the world I came from?

Argentinosaurus

This tiny terror is Microraptor. It is just 40–60 centimetres long

Being small helps me to glide from trees.

Where did they live?

The first dinosaurs lived on Pangaea – a single, giant slab of land. The world was very hot and dry and there was just one ocean called Panthalassa. Dinosaurs could walk all the way from the North Pole to the South Pole. We call this time in Earth's history the Triassic.

PANGAEA

Who would be at a dino party?

Dinosaurs were reptiles, so they might invite other reptiles. These baby *Maiasaura* have just hatched, so they are sharing their birthday party. Can you spot which guests are not dinosaurs?

Maiasaura

Who looked after the babies?

Maiasaura mums took good care of their nests, eggs and young. They protected them from hungry *Troodon*.

Watch out kids, that hungry Troodon has its big eyes on you!

Troodon was an intelligent dinosaur with big eyes and sharp claws

Why do dinos have such strange names?

Dinosaur names are often made up of more than one word. Put together, the words tell us more about the dinosaur.

Carcharodontosaurus shark-tooth-lizard

Tyrannosaurus rex tyrant-lizard-king

Guanlong crown-dragon

Maiasaura good mother-lizard

Triceratops three-horned-face

Torosaurus bull-lizard

Mei long sleeping-dragon

Hey, who is Tyrannosaurus rex?

Mei long was covered in bird-like feathers and may have been very colourful

Did dinosaurs have fur?

No, dinosaurs didn't have fur but many of them had feathers. The feathers were often fluffy, but some dinosaurs grew long feathers, like modern birds. Fuzzy, fluffy feathers kept dinosaurs warm.

Yutyrannus was up to 9 metres long and covered in fuzzy feathers

Did you know?

A fully-grown *T rex* was **longer** and **heavier** than a bus and its skull was so heavy you'd need a forklift truck to pick it up.

In 1824 **Megalosaurus** was the first dinosaur to be named. When its thighbone was dug up people thought it belonged to a human giant!

Meat-eating dinosaurs had long, curved, sharp teeth.

Titanosaurs were huge, long-necked dinosaurs but they were not the largest animals to ever live. The **blue whale**, which lives in our oceans today, wins that prize.

Plant-eaters had peg-like or spoon-shaped teeth.

All dinos could **walk**, some of them could **swim** and others – like *Microraptor* – could **glide** between trees.

Dinosaurs didn't have **kneecaps**, but no one knows why!

T rex and *Tarbosaurus* might have made good **ballet dancers** – they balanced beautifully on their tiptoes!

Ichthyosaurs were fast-swimming reptiles that lived in the sea. They looked like whales or dolphins, but were related to **snakes** and **lizards**.

Which dinosaurs had the longest necks?

Sauropods were a group of huge dinosaurs with very long necks, like *Brachiosaurus*. Having a long neck meant that sauropods could reach high up into trees to eat leaves. They might spend all day eating.

Mamenchisaurus had a long, thin neck that was 12 metres in length

Mamenchisaurus

Brachiosaurus

Parasaurolophus

Could dinosaurs roaaarr?

No one knows what sounds dinosaurs made. They may have roared, growled, chirped, tweeted – or made no sounds at all. *Parasaurolophus* had a long, hollow crest on its head. It may have blown air through the crest to make honking sounds – like a trumpet!

Diplodocus

Diplodocus *had a long, bendy tail too, which it used to wallop other dinosaurs*

Do you think I'm handsome?

Oviraptor

Some dinosaurs liked to look good! Horns, frills, head plates and colourful feathers or skin may have all helped male dinosaurs look attractive to female ones.

Who was king of the dinosaurs?

Look out! Here comes *Tyrannosaurus rex* – king of the dinosaurs. *T rex* was a massive 13 metres long and weighed about 7 tonnes – that makes it one of the biggest meat-eaters that's ever lived on land, in the whole history of the planet!

T rex may have hunted in groups. A pack of them would have been a terrifying sight for a Triceratops like me!

Yikes!

How scary was a T rex?

T rex was one of the scariest dinosaurs to ever live. It was a huge, fearsome, powerful hunter that preyed on other big dinosaurs. It could bite its prey so hard it snapped bones.

Sharp claws on hands and feet

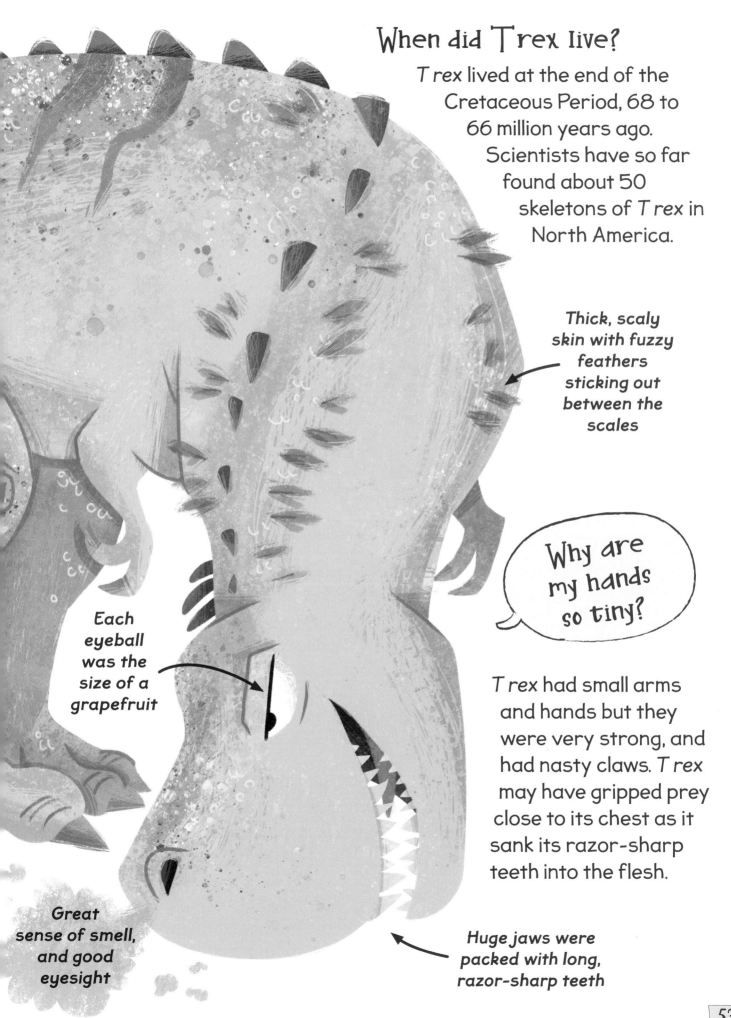

When did T rex live?

T rex lived at the end of the Cretaceous Period, 68 to 66 million years ago. Scientists have so far found about 50 skeletons of T rex in North America.

Thick, scaly skin with fuzzy feathers sticking out between the scales

Why are my hands so tiny?

T rex had small arms and hands but they were very strong, and had nasty claws. T rex may have gripped prey close to its chest as it sank its razor-sharp teeth into the flesh.

Each eyeball was the size of a grapefruit

Great sense of smell, and good eyesight

Huge jaws were packed with long, razor-sharp teeth

How many?

3

The number of claws *Therizinosaurus* had on each hand – the longest was 71 centimetres long! It probably used its claws to grab branches and pull leaves to its mouth.

10

The size in centimetres of the smallest known dinosaur eggs. The biggest were 30 centimetres long – twice as big as an ostrich egg.

50

The number of new species of dinosaur being discovered every year.

In 1905 the bones of a *T rex* were put on display in a museum for the first time. Scientists thought they were just **8 million** years old!

T rex could run at speeds of about **30** kilometres an hour – that's faster than an elephant but much slower than a racehorse.

Most dinos probably grew quickly and died before they reached the age of **30**.

The world was about **6°C** hotter during the Cretaceous than it is today. The hot, steamy weather meant that lush forests could grow as far as the North Pole!

19 The number of bones in the neck of Mamenchisaurus – more than any dinosaur discovered so far.

2 The weight in kilograms that a 10-year-old *T rex* would have gained every day! A newly hatched *T rex* would have been the size of pigeon, but it grew super fast.

The Jurassic Period lasted **55 million years**. Then Pangaea began to break up into big chunks of land called continents.

How did dinosaurs defend themselves?

Many plant-eating dinosaurs had bony armour to protect them from attack. Thick slabs of bone, plates, scales, spikes and bony bumps all helped ankylosaurs fend off the razor-sharp claws and dagger-like teeth of meat-eating dinosaurs.

Why is there a big club on your tail?

Smash!

Ankylosaurus

I'm an ankylosaur from the Late Cretaceous. I have a huge club on the end of my tail and it's very useful for walloping anything that attacks me — like that Trex over there!

Trex

Roar!

Why did Triceratops have horns?

i use my long horns to defend myself against Trex and other big predators. i can raise the big bony frill around my neck to make myself look scarier too!

i'm a bonehead dinosaur. My skull is 25 centimetres thick. i can use it to batter my rivals, and it makes me look cool too!

Why is your head so big?

Bonehead dinosaurs used their big heads to ram into each other

Pachycephalosaurus

Crash!

57

What did dinosaurs eat?

Some dinosaurs hunted animals to eat, other dinosaurs ate plants, and some ate whatever they could find!

i'm fully armed with slashing, gripping claws and jaws lined with razor-sharp teeth. i'm fast, smart... and hungry for meat!

Raptors, like Deinonychus, were light on their feet and super speedy

Sauropelta

i eat plants. My body is covered in bony plates and spikes that make it difficult for Deinonychus to attack me!

How much did T rex eat?

Yum!

T rex was a hungry beast that needed about 110 kilograms of meat a day. That's more than 1000 burgers!

Plant-eaters like me graze on low-growing plants and leaves. Even our teeth are shaped like leaves!

I look like an ostrich with my long legs, feathers and toothless beak. I mostly peck at bugs, lizards and other small animals.

Deinonychus

Ornithomimus

How fast could a dinosaur run?

Plant-eating dinosaurs were slow movers, but most predator dinosaurs needed speed to hunt and catch their prey.

Ornithomimus was *one of the fastest dinosaurs, with top speeds of 35 kilometres an hour or more*

Could dinosaurs fly?

Yes, and they still do! Flying dinosaurs are all around us. We call them birds.

Over a long time, some dinosaurs began to develop bird-like bodies with wings and feathers. By 150 million years ago, the first birds had appeared. That means all birds are actually dinosaurs!

What was the first bird called?

Archaeopteryx – that's me! I have teeth, claws on my wings and a long, bony tail. I can climb, run, glide and even fly a little.

I lived 130 million years ago. I could glide between trees and flap my wings.

Microraptor

Quetzalcoatlus

I'm a giant pterosaur. I have a wingspan of 12 metres and I'm one of the biggest animals to ever fly – one of my feet is bigger than a human's leg!

What is a pterosaur?

Pterosaurs were flying reptiles that lived at the same time as the dinosaurs. Their wings were made of thin skin, spread out between the bones in their arms and fingers, and they were superb flyers.

Would you rather?

Have a **Maiasaura** or **Majungatholus** for a mum? Scientists think that *Majungatholus* may have eaten members of its own family!

Fight a *T rex* or **fly** with a pterosaur?

Be a **fast-running** Gallimimus or a **slow-moving** Stegosaurus?

Have **teeth** like *T rex* or a **neck** like *Supersaurus*? You'd either need a very big toothbrush, or a very long scarf!

If you had the body of a sauropod would you use your long tail to **splash** in water, or let people **slide** down it?

Be as **big** as Brachiosaurus or as **small** as Microraptor?

Be covered in a coat of **soft, fluffy feathers** or have **scary horns** growing on your face?

Have tea with a *Tarbosaurus*, **cuddle** a *Carcharodontosaurus* or **stroke** a *Stegosaurus*?

63

How could sauropods grow so big?

Sauropods were giant plant-eaters. They had big bones and huge muscles to move their bodies. They also had holes and air sacs in their bones, which kept them light. Without these, sauropods would have been even heavier!

Could a dinosaur crush a car?

Argentinosaurus weighed over 60 tonnes. If it sat on a car, it could crush it in an instant! *T rex* had one of the most powerful bites of any animal ever known. It could have crushed a car in its mighty jaws!

Crunch!

Brachiosaurus

I am three times taller than a giraffe!

How did dinosaurs kill their prey?

They were equipped with some lethal weapons! Claws, jaws, teeth and tails could all be used to injure, catch or kill other animals. Raptors had long, curved claws on their feet for slashing and slicing.

What happened to the dinosaurs?

After more than 150 million years of ruling the world, disaster struck the dinosaurs. An enormous space rock, called an asteroid, smashed into Earth.

How did Earth change?

It turned cold and dark, and there was very little food because plants couldn't grow. Over the next few thousand years, most types of animals, including the dinosaurs, went extinct.

The dinosaurs began to die, along with many other animals

The asteroid hit Earth with the explosive force of a billion giant bombs

There were giant waves, floods and burning winds before dark clouds of dust filled the sky

Are the dinosaurs still alive?

Yes they are! Birds belong to the dinosaur family, and some survived the asteroid, along with other animals. Today, more than 10,000 different types of bird live all over the world.

Eagles have sharp claws and beaks like many dinosaurs did

Can you believe I'm a dinosaur? RAAA!

Huge, flightless terror birds lived in South America about two million years ago

Ducks, geese and chickens are dinosaur relatives

Who collects dino poo?

① This dinosaur died and its soft parts rotted away

We do! We're palaeontologists (say: pal-ee-on-tol-oh-jists). We look for the remains of animals that lived long ago.

What's a fossil?

A fossil is the remains of an animal that has turned to stone over millions of years.

② Its bones were covered in sand or mud

We look at fossils of bones and footprints. Fossil poo helps us to work out what dinosaurs ate.

Where can I find dinosaurs?

Lots of museums have dinosaur fossils you can look at. They are being dug up all over the world, from the USA to China! Mudstone, sandstone and limestone are all good rocks in which to find fossils.

Whose tooth is that?

It's a fossilized tooth from a Trex! Each adult had 50 massive teeth and they could grow new ones if the old ones fell out or broke.

③ Over time, the bones were buried by more sand or mud and turned to stone – they have been fossilized

My bones are revealed when land erodes (wears away).

A compendium of questions

My huge body is built for hunting!

It may have been the super scary *Spinosaurus*. It was probably longer and heavier than *T rex*, and its huge head had crocodile-like jaws lined with teeth.

Were dinosaurs clever?

Some were! *Troodon* had a big brain for its size. It was smarter than a turtle but not as clever as a parrot.

Why did Brachiosaurus eat stones?

Like many reptiles, *Brachiosaurus* probably swallowed stones to help grind up tough plant food in its stomach.

How many types of dinosaur are there?

How many dinosaurs can you name?

About 2000 types have been found and named so far, but there are plenty more to discover.

Were pterosaurs flying dinosaurs?

Pterosaurs could fly but they were not dinosaurs. They belonged to a group of reptiles that appeared before the first dinosaurs.

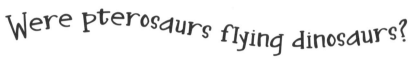

Could I out-run a Velociraptor?

No! *Velociraptor* could reach speeds of 35 kilometres an hour. Few animals could escape those razor-sharp claws!

Which dinosaur loved stinky smells?

Tarbosaurus was a hunter, but also ate dead animals that it found by following the stench of rotting flesh.

Which dino could fish?

Deinocheirus could. It had very long arms and sharp claws. It may have reached into rivers to grab fish or reached high into trees to pick fruit.

Were any dinosaurs friendly?

Some dinosaurs, like *Iguanodon*, probably lived peacefully in herds. *T rex* might have hunted in packs, but was probably not friendly!

What colour are your eyes?

If you could have an extra sense, what would it be?

My Body

Do you go to bed early or late?

How tall are you?

What is my body for?

Your body lets you see, hear, smell, taste and touch the world around you. You can use it to run, jump, think, talk, and have all kinds of fun. Without it, you couldn't do anything.

> Our bodies look different on the outside, but inside we all have bones, muscles and blood.

> Cells make up tissue such as bone, muscle and blood.

Why are cells so special?

Because they are the tiny building blocks that together make up your body. Different cells do different jobs. You have blood cells, bone cells, skin cells and lots more.

Bone cells make up your skeleton

X-rays can check for broken bones.

How can doctors see inside our bodies?

Doctors can look inside the body with scans and X-rays to see where all the parts are and how they fit together. They can even look at single cells with microscopes that magnify them.

Muscle cells help to form every muscle in your body

Your blood contains trillions of red blood cells

Why do I need to eat?

Food provides the energy your body needs to keep working. Chemicals from food repair your body and help it grow. Your body breaks down food and rearranges the chemicals to make skin, hair, bones and all the other parts.

Can I balance my food?

Yes you can, but not on your head! It's important to eat a wide range of foods from different food groups to make sure you stay fit and healthy.

Fruit and vegetables
Eat lots of these for fibre and goodness

Protein
Meat, fish and beans help your body grow and repair itself

What happens when i eat?

The food you eat takes a long and twisty route through your digestive system. At each stage, your body pulls out the good things it needs.

Always wash your hands before eating.

① How do teeth help?

Your teeth break up food as you chew. They chew it into smaller pieces and mash it around. Food mixes with saliva in your mouth, making it easier to swallow.

② Where does food go first?

When you swallow, food goes into a tube in your throat called your oesophagus (say 'ee-sof-a-guss'). Muscles push the food down to your stomach, squeezing behind the lump of food so that it moves along.

Oesophagus

From mouth to stomach takes 5–8 seconds

⑤ Why do I need to poo?

To get rid of the bits that your body doesn't need. These parts are squashed together and mixed with dead cells and water from your gut. They leave your body when you go to the toilet.

Always wash your hands after going to the toilet.

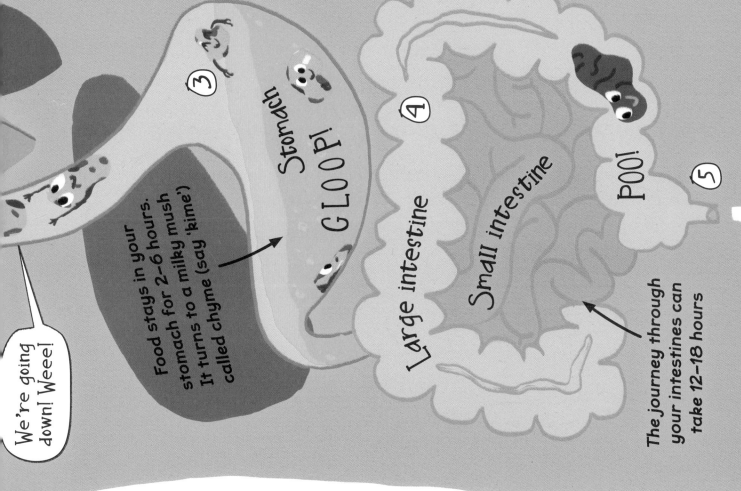

We're going down! Weee!

Food stays in your stomach for 2–6 hours. It turns to a milky mush called chyme (say 'kime')

③

Stomach
GLOOP!

④
Large intestine

Small intestine

POO!

⑤

The journey through your intestines can take 12–18 hours

③ Why is there acid in my stomach?

Acid dissolves food into a gloopy liquid. Muscles in your stomach also churn the mixture around to break it up.

④ What goes on in my intestines?

A milky mushy liquid moves into and through your intestines where nutrients (useful chemicals) and water are absorbed. The leftover parts are turned into... poo!

How many?

35 The number of tonnes of food the average person eats in their life.

110,000 The number of hairs on the head of a dark-haired person; blondes have more and redheads have fewer.

37 trillion The number of human cells in an adult body.

1.5–2 The area in square metres of an adult's skin.

0.5 The volume of gas in litres that your gut produces each day.

69 The largest number of babies anyone has had.

Your nose can detect **1 trillion** smells.

16 The speed in kilometres per hour of a sneeze.

A hair grows **1.25** centimetres each month.

900 The length in centimetres of the longest-ever fingernail.

120 The speed in metres per second of a message travelling along a nerve.

5 The amount in litres of blood in an average adult human.

The length in millimetres of your smallest bone (it's inside your ear). **3**

What is my skeleton made of?

Bones form the rigid framework for your body – your skeleton. They support your body and provide somewhere for your muscles to fix to.

Imagine how floppy and blobby you'd be without bones!

Skull

Clavicle

Jaw

Ribs

Humerus

Sternum

Spine

Ulna

Radius

Pelvis

Femur

Patella

How do muscles move me?

Most muscles are fixed to your bones. As they contract, they pull the bones along with them, moving your body. Being active makes your muscles strong. Run, swim, jump, cycle – do anything you like!

Biceps muscle contracts to bend your arm

contract

relax

Fibula

Tibia

Tendon attaches muscle to bone

Triceps muscle relaxes

Phalanges

Which muscle works the hardest?

Your heart works harder than any other muscle. It never stops pumping blood around your body throughout your life.

I need exercise too! It helps to make me strong.

Knee joint

Ankle joint

Activities like dancing are good for getting your heart working.

Hip joint

Joints make you flexible, you couldn't move without them.

Elbow joint

Wrist joint

How does my body bend?

You have lots of joints in your body such as in your knees, elbows, shoulders, ankles and wrists. These are places where bones meet, and they allow your body to bend or move in different ways.

Activities like swimming make you breathe fast

Lung

Heart

Lung

What happens when I breathe?

When you breathe in, your lungs fill with air. Oxygen from the air goes into your blood and is delivered to your whole body. Old air is pushed out when you breathe out.

How does my blood deliver oxygen?

Your blood flows through tubes called blood vessels. These reach every single part of your body to make sure you have all the oxygen you need. Your heart and blood together are called the circulatory system.

Blood vessels

Why does my heart thump?

When you exercise, your heart beats faster to pump blood around your body quickly, to deliver the oxygen your muscles need. You also breathe faster to get more oxygen, and you feel out of breath.

Why can't i breathe underwater?

Because you don't have gills like a fish! Your lungs can only take oxygen from the air. A fish's gills can take dissolved oxygen from water. When you swim underwater, you need to come to the surface for air.

Why am I ticklish?

Because you have a sense of touch! Your body uses five senses to find out about the world around you. Your senses pick up information and send it to your brain.

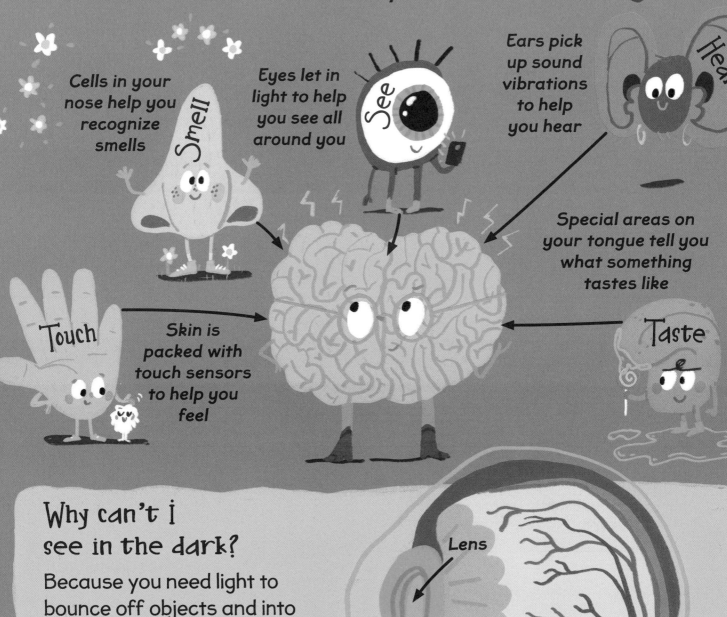

Cells in your nose help you recognize smells

Smell

Eyes let in light to help you see all around you

See

Ears pick up sound vibrations to help you hear

Hear

Special areas on your tongue tell you what something tastes like

Touch

Skin is packed with touch sensors to help you feel

Taste

Why can't I see in the dark?

Because you need light to bounce off objects and into your eyes. A lens in your eye helps focus the light, and a nerve carries information to your brain to make an image — and that is what you see.

Lens

Optic nerve to brain

Why are ears a funny shape?

The shape of your ears helps to funnel sound into them. Sound is then carried inside your ear, where signals are sent along a nerve to your brain, so it can make sense of what you hear.

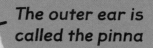

The outer ear is called the pinna

Tiny ear bones

Soundwaves in

Auditory nerve to brain

How do I smell?

Your sense of smell is produced by cells high above and behind your nose. Tiny particles of the thing you are smelling reach those cells.

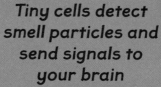

Tiny cells detect smell particles and send signals to your brain

Smell particles go up your nose

What helps me taste food?

Your tongue is covered with blobs surrounded by tiny taste buds. The taste buds send messages to your brain about the chemicals dissolved in food, and your brain turns the information into tastes.

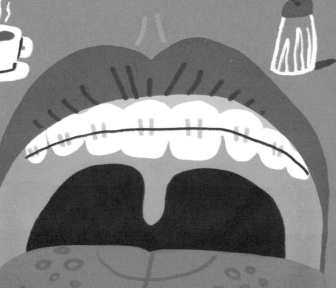

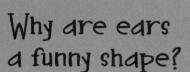

Did you know?

Your **teeth** are as strong as a **shark's** teeth – but your jaws are smaller so you can't bite like a shark.

Babies can hear before they're born, though sounds from the outside are a bit **muffled**.

I hope I grow up to be a better singer than Mum.

An **adult** can survive three weeks without **food**, but only about four days without **water**.

Your **ears** are important to your sense of **balance**.

In **complete darkness**, your eyes could spot the light from a candle 48 kilometres away.

Some parts of your body are never replaced. The **enamel** on your teeth and the **goo** inside your **eyes** have to last a lifetime.

By the time you were six months old, your **eyes** were already **two thirds** their adult size.

Hi. Hi. Hi.

Hi Hi

Children can hear higher sounds than adults, including **bats** squeaking and **ultrasonic** dog whistles.

Fingerprints are not the body's only unique pattern. You can also be identified by your **tongue print**, your personal **smell** and the pattern in your **iris** (the coloured part of your eye).

Your **blood** is made inside your **bones**.

Is my brain in charge?

What you say, think and how you move, and everything else you do, is controlled by your brain.

It receives information

A network of nerves tells your brain what is happening to your body. Your brain is linked to your body by your spinal cord

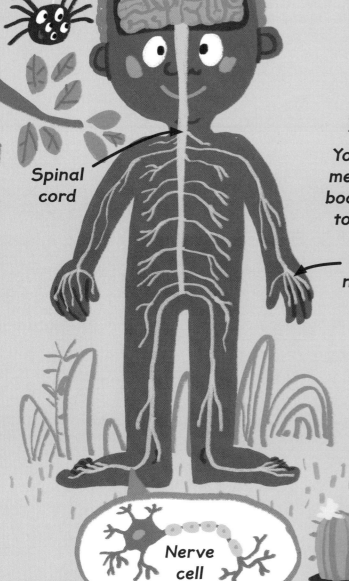

Brain

Spinal cord

Nerve network

It sends messages

Your brain sends messages to your body, telling it how to react or move

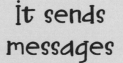

Stand on one foot and spin the ball.

What do my nerves do?

Nerves are collections of nerve cells (neurons). They carry information between all parts of your body and brain. When you see, smell, taste or hear anything, information is carried by nerves to your brain super-quickly.

Nerve cell

5

Your brain is protected by your skull, and a layer of fluid

Think and plan

Touch and taste

Talk and smell

Hear

See

Move

Different areas of your brain control different things

How do i remember things?

Everything is stored in your brain, including memories, dreams and what you've learnt at school. Your brain stores some information for just seconds, and some for a lifetime.

④

Why do we say 'ouch'?

If you touch something hot, nerves carry signals to your spinal cord (1). This responds immediately (2) and sends a message through other nerves to make your hand move away (3). A slower message goes to your brain (4) that makes you feel pain and say 'ouch'.

①

Spinal cord

②

③

Why do I sleep?

Your body uses the time you're asleep to repair any injuries, grow, rest and sort out what you've experienced and learnt during the day. No one knows exactly how sleep works, but we do know that we can't live without it.

Does everyone dream?

Yes, but not everyone remembers their dreams. Most people have 3–5 dreams each night. Even cats and dogs have dreams!

No one knows what animals dream about!

Why are dreams so weird?

As your brain sorts through information while you sleep, it's in a jumbled order, with recent events mixed up with old memories. Some people think secret meanings are hidden in dreams.

Each dream can last 20 minutes or a few seconds

How much sleep do I need?

We need different amounts of sleep at different ages. Newborn babies sleep for a long time every day. Adults sleep less.

Hours
18
16
14
12
10
8
6
4
2
0

Newborn   Pre-school   School   Teen   Adult

Would you rather?

Be able to breathe underwater or be **light** enough to walk on top of the water?

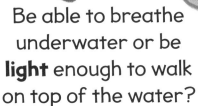

Have a really long **tongue** or really long **fingers**?

Have **super-keen sight** or be able to hear very **quiet sounds** like ants munching their food?

Grow really long **fingernails** or really **long hair**?

Have **unbreakable** bones or **uncuttable** skin?

Have **wings** or a **tail**?

Be **wobbly** like a jellyfish with no bones, or have a **hard** outer shell like a tortoise?

Be entirely **furry** or entirely **bald**?

Have eyes in the back of your **head** or in the tips of your **fingers**?

Be able to run really **fast** or for a really **long** time?

Where do babies come from?

Babies come from inside their mum's body. A baby grows in the mum's uterus, where it gets everything it needs until it's ready to be born.

Cord

Uterus

I can feel the baby kicking!

Goodness from the mother's food is carried along the cord to the baby

Egg cell divides again and again

Day 1

Day 2

Days 3–4

How fast does a baby grow?

Inside its mum, a baby grows really fast. It starts off as a tiny egg, which divides to make the billions of cells that make up the whole baby. After nine months, the baby is big enough to be born.

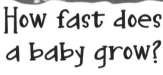

12 weeks
5 centimetres

20 weeks
16 centimetres

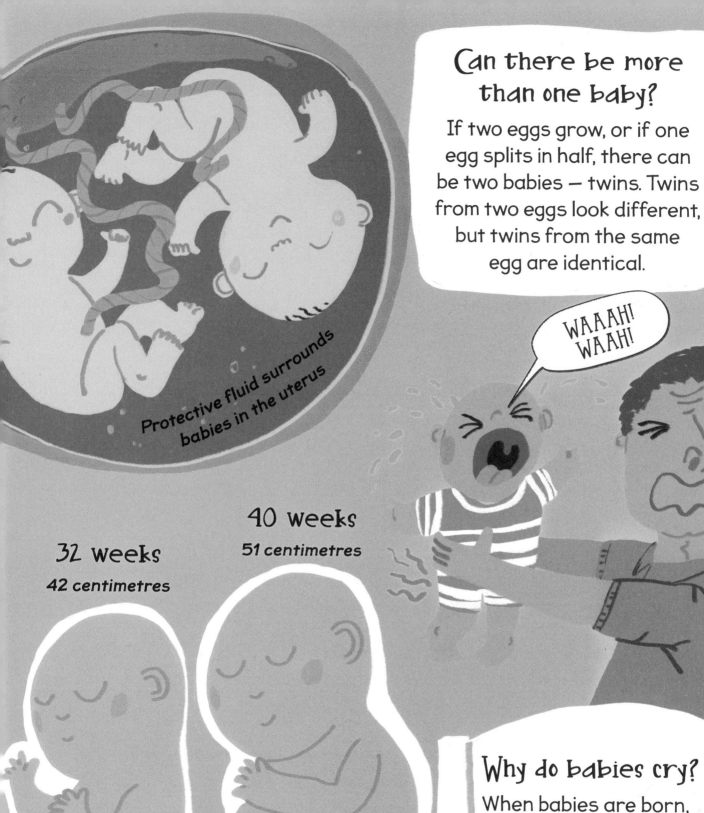

Can there be more than one baby?

If two eggs grow, or if one egg splits in half, there can be two babies — twins. Twins from two eggs look different, but twins from the same egg are identical.

Protective fluid surrounds babies in the uterus

WAAAH! WAAH!

32 weeks
42 centimetres

40 weeks
51 centimetres

Why do babies cry?

When babies are born, they can't talk or do anything for themselves. They cry to tell their parents that they're hungry, or they're cold — or that their nappy needs changing!

Am I always growing?

You keep growing from when you are born until your late teens or early twenties. But the speed you grow at slows down. A baby triples its weight in a year.

> Do you know how tall you are?

5 years

> Babies double their weight in five months. If you kept doing that you'd be huge!

6 months

10 years

Newborn

How do I get taller?

A soft, flexible substance called cartilage grows inside your bones, making them longer. The cartilage slowly hardens into bone.

Cartilage hardens to bone

Why does my hair need cutting?

Your hair grows throughout your life, so you have to keep cutting it. Hair grows from a little pit on your scalp called a hair follicle, but the hair you can see is actually dead. That's why it doesn't hurt to have a haircut.

Hair follicle

15 years

20 years

70 years

Your ears keep getting bigger too, but very slowly.

Grandma? Grandpa?

Do we shrink as we get older?

Yes! The bones of the spine get squashed closer together over the years. Some older people also get a curved spine and stoop, and that makes them look even shorter.

A compendium of questions

What are goosebumps?

They are bumps on your skin where tiny muscles make your hairs stand up if you are cold or scared.

Why do my first teeth fall out?

Your first teeth are temporary — you have them until your mouth grows large enough for your permanent teeth. You have 20 first teeth, and they are replaced by larger, stronger, teeth.

Your permanent teeth need to last your whole life, so it's important to look after them!

What are hiccups?

If the muscle across your chest suddenly squeezes, it can snap shut the opening to your vocal flaps, making the 'hic' sound.

Why do we like sugar if it's bad for us?

Millions of years ago, our ancestors ate a sugar-rich fruit diet. So gradually people grew to like sweet things.

Why do I yawn?

No one's quite sure, but possibly as a way of getting more oxygen into your body quickly.

Why do we get wrinkles?

As skin ages, it loses its elasticity, so it can't spring back into shape after stretching (such as when you smile).

Why don't I have to remember to breathe?

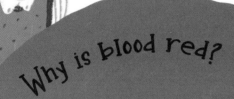

Why is blood red?

Blood contains a chemical for carrying oxygen that contains iron. When this chemical picks up oxygen, it turns redder.

My knee hurts now, but soon I'll have a scab!

What makes a scab?

When your blood meets the air, special cells called platelets break up and mix with a protein in blood to make tangly fibres, forming a scab.

Your brain deals with all kinds of automatic activities without you having to think about them, including breathing, and digesting food.

What is my tummy button for?

When you were inside your mother, you got nutrients and oxygen through the umbilical cord that connected you to her body. The tummy button is what's left after the cord is cut.

Why do I sleep more when I'm ill?

Your body needs energy to fight the illness, so to save energy it makes you sleep.

Why is our planet in peril?

Our beautiful planet is in peril because we haven't been taking good care of it. Earth is a precious home for all of us, and the plants and animals that live here too.

How many people are on the planet?

There are more than 7.7 billion people. That's 7,700,000,000 humans! Every one of us has an important job to do. Let's work together to save the Earth!

What is air?

The air is made up of gases and it's wrapped around Earth like a snug blanket. It's called the atmosphere.

21% oxygen

78% nitrogen

1% other gases, including carbon dioxide

Humans breathe in oxygen and breathe out carbon dioxide.

A gas called nitrogen makes up most of the atmosphere. Which gas makes up the next biggest part of the atmosphere?

Plants' leaves take in carbon dioxide to make food. They give out oxygen.

Why does Earth need a blanket?

A blanket of air keeps our planet the perfect temperature!

1 As the Sun's energy reaches Earth's atmosphere, some of it travels through and warms the surface

2 Earth's surface releases heat and some of it escapes back into space

3 Gases in the atmosphere trap some of the heat and reflect it back to Earth, keeping our planet a lovely warm place to live. This is called the greenhouse effect

The gases in the atmosphere that trap the heat, such as carbon dioxide and methane, are called greenhouse gases.

Atmosphere

The world's oceans are warming up and melting my icy Arctic home.

Is Earth getting hotter?

Yes! Things humans do are creating more greenhouse gases. This means that more heat is trapped, so Earth is getting too warm. This is called global warming. Our weather is being affected – we call that climate change.

Did you know?

Carbon dioxide

Plants are great at mopping up extra **carbon dioxide** and pumping lots of **oxygen** into the air! That's why we need forests, fields and parks.

Oxygen

If we didn't have an **atmosphere** there would be no air to breathe, and Earth's average temperature would be a very chilly −6°C!

There are more than one billion **cows** in the world, and almost all of them are kept on farms. They all make greenhouse gases when they fart and burp.

Sometimes Earth is called the **Goldilocks planet** because its distance from the Sun means it's just the right temperature for us.

Too hot!   Just right!   Too cold!

5000 TODAY!

You can plant a **tree** to help keep Earth's atmosphere healthy. Some trees are more than 5000 years old.

Scientists looked at how hot the Earth was in the last 100 years and found the five **hottest** years have been since 2010.

Trees can be used to make all of these things: soap, shampoo, rubber gloves, chocolate, paper, clothes and medicines. When trees are cut down, it's important that new ones are planted.

Plants make perfect **presents** for people who care about the planet!

If you lined up all the **cars** in the world they could stretch round it 40 times! Think of all the dirty gases they are putting in the air, and leave your car at home whenever you can!

Trains are a greener way to travel than planes because they make up to six times less dirty gas.

We are taking too many **fish** from the sea. Some fishing nets are more than 60 metres wide and can trap tens of thousands of fish at a time.

What is dirty energy?

Burning oil, gas, wood and coal gives us energy to power our homes and vehicles. This puts more greenhouse gases in the air, and causes pollution.

Pollution is something in the environment that is harmful or poisonous.

Oil, gas and coal are called fossil fuels because they formed inside Earth long ago, from dead animals and plants!

Smoke containing harmful gases

This power station is burning coal. Most air pollution comes from burning fossil fuels

This cycle lane is made up of solar panels. They use the Sun's energy to make electricity for lots of people.

How can bikes help us save the planet?

Cycling, skate-boarding and walking are clean, green ways to get around. You can travel one kilometre by bike in about three minutes, by skateboard in about six minutes, or on foot in about 10 minutes.

Solar panels

What is clean energy?

Not all power comes from dirty fossil fuels. The great news is that there are loads of ways of making clean, green energy!

Wind turbines can turn wind energy into electricity, or other types of power

Wind power

The energy of flowing water can be used to make hydroelectric power

Hydroelectric Power

Some countries are situated over superhot parts of the Earth. They can use underground heat to produce electricity. It's called geothermal power

Geothermal power

How can I save energy?

Saving energy is one of the best ways to be green. You can:

Dry your washing outside instead of using a tumble dryer.

Put on warm clothes instead of turning the heating up.

Turn off lights when you are not in the room and unplug chargers.

Can you think of other ways to save energy at home and school?

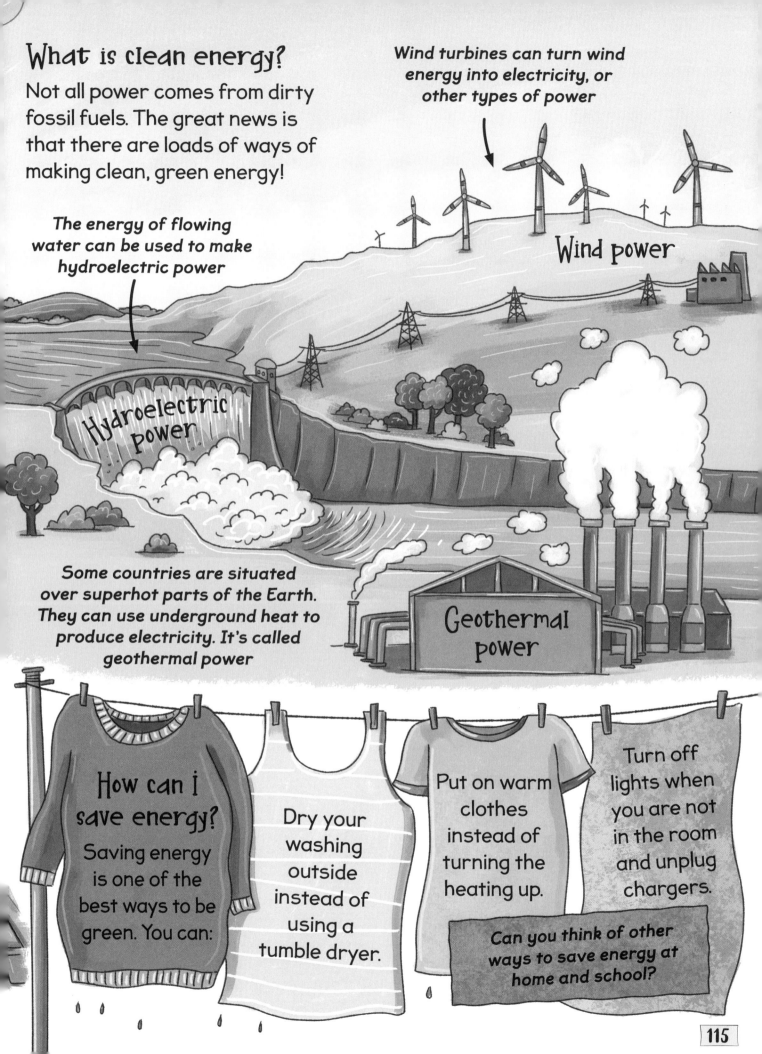

Why are jellyfish blooming?

Jellyfish love warm water, and as the world's oceans get warmer, the number of jellyfish is rising. Large numbers can even form massive groups, or blooms. The fish aren't so happy, as jellyfish eat them!

Seals that normally eat the fish now have less food. The damage we do to our planet affects all living things.

Why did my colourful home turn white?

Coral reefs need clean, warm water to survive. When the water gets too hot, or dirty, the coral animals die, and the reef turns white.

Why are the oceans dirty?

Our oceans are dirtier than ever because lots of plastic waste has been dumped in the water. Plastic in the ocean gets broken down into tiny pieces, and animals eat them.

How can I help turtles?

Some turtles try to eat plastic bags floating in the sea. They think the bags are their favourite food – jellyfish – and the plastic kills them.

Join a seaside clean-up to help keep beaches clean.

Always take your rubbish home and recycle as much of it as you can.

Ask for paper straws instead of plastic ones, which often end up in the sea.

You can help us turtles and other sea creatures by using canvas or long-life shopping bags instead of plastic ones.

When you go on holiday, don't buy souvenirs that are made from animals or their homes.

How many?

More than **80** countries already use wind power to produce electricity.

In Japan, people use wooden chopsticks to eat. Every year, they get through **90,000** tonnes of them! Can you think of some fun ways to reuse chopsticks?

1

The number of drinks cans you need to recycle to save energy for **4** hours of TV.

There is so much heat deep inside Earth that it could provide us with enough power for **1,000,000** years!

Make sure all your light bulbs are the new energy-saving ones. They last up to **15** times longer and can be recycled!

640

The number of litres of water a garden sprinkler uses in an hour. Use a watering can instead!

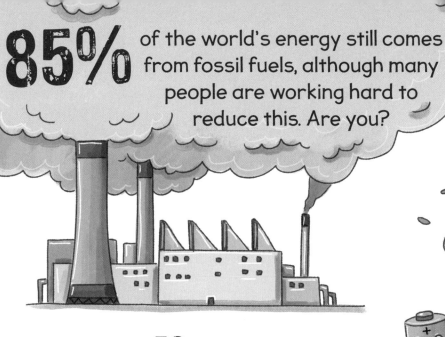

85% of the world's energy still comes from fossil fuels, although many people are working hard to reduce this. Are you?

100 The number of trees you could save from being cut down if your whole class recycle paper for a year.

It takes **50** times as much energy to make a battery as there is stored in the battery! Use rechargeable batteries whenever you can.

The Great Pacific Garbage Patch, a mass of litter floating in the North Pacific Ocean, covers around **1.6 million** square kilometres.

Pacific Ocean

10

The number of litres of clean water in a toilet flush.

Only **3%** of the water on Earth is fresh (not salty), and most of that is frozen. This is why we need to save water where we can.

Where does wee go?

All of the waste water from our homes gets carried away in underground pipes. They're called sewers.

Why are showers best?

A bath uses about 80 litres of water, but a shower uses about 40 litres instead.

Cleaning water uses lots of energy. Turn off the tap while you are brushing your teeth. Can you think of other ways to save water?

That stinks!

Sewers carry the waste water to a place where it is cleaned so it can be used again

Some sewers also collect rainwater. If the sewer overflows, it empties into rivers or the ocean!

How can I help keep rivers healthy?

• Never throw rubbish into a river
• Never release pet fish or other animals into a river
• Find out about organic food. When farmers grow organic food they use fewer chemicals that pollute rivers

The place where sewage is cleaned and the water recycled is called a sewage plant

In special tanks, the solid waste and nasty bugs are taken out

The solids that are removed can also be recycled!

The cleaned water is put into rivers, streams, or the ocean

These types of pollution damage rivers:

Rubbish

Harmful chemicals from farms and factories

Raw sewage (that's poo and wee!)

Some parts of the world have no sewage plants, so raw sewage flows into rivers or the ocean.

121

How far did my banana travel?

The distance food travels from where it was grown, to where it will be eaten, is measured in food miles.

1

This banana travelled by truck to get to a boat

50 miles

2

Then it crossed an ocean

5000 miles

3

Then it was put on a lorry and taken to a supermarket

70 miles

4

We bought it and it travelled in our car to get to our home

5 miles

5

It came with me on my bike to school

How many food miles does this banana have? Which part of its journey used the least energy?

2 miles

How can food waste be turned into energy?

When food rots it gives off methane. This can be collected and used for cooking, or heating homes. Plant waste can also be used to make fuel for cars.

4 The methane is used to power electricity generators

5 Electricity is supplied to homes

3 Bacteria in the tank eat the waste, which gives off methane as it breaks down

Methane can also be collected from my poo!

1 Food waste is collected from homes, supermarkets and restaurants

2 All the waste goes in a special sealed tank, where no oxygen can reach it

Who has green fingers?

I do! I grow fruit and veg in my garden so these foods have no food miles!

I put the compost on my garden to help new plants grow. Thanks worms!

Why are worms really useful?

We munch up leftover food, peelings, eggshells and garden waste. We turn it into compost.

123

Would you rather?

Would you rather save water by sharing a **bath** with your dog, or by giving yourself a time limit on your **showers**?

You want to recycle your old toys. Would you rather take them to a **charity shop**, or **swap** them with a friend?

If you get cold, would you rather warm up by **running** on the spot or by wearing a big **jumper**?

Would you rather be a wriggly worm eating **rotten food** in a compost heap, or a dung beetle munching on **elephant poo**?

Would you rather try to make a **space rocket** from cans, or a **submarine** from a plastic bottle?

If you worked in a safari park, would you rather **teach** people about nature... or **check** a crocodile's teeth?

You want to cut down your food miles. Would you rather catch your own **fish**, keep your own **hens**, or grow your own **tomatoes**?

Which environment would you most like to work to protect – the **Amazon rainforest** or the chilly **North Pole**?

What is an animal's home called?

The place where an animal lives is called a habitat. Forests, grasslands, rivers and deserts are types of habitat. When habitats are destroyed, some animals lose their homes, and might go extinct.

Bornean orang-utan

Where did your home go?

In Borneo, diverse forests the size of 180 football pitches are cut down every hour so palm trees can be grown. Avoid buying foods made with palm oil and you can help us keep our homes.

Bengal tiger

How can you help to save animal habitats?

Wildlife charities work to save habitats, and raising money for them is a good way to help. It's also a good idea to only buy food and products that have been made without harming wild habitats.

I'm doing a sponsored silence to raise money to protect wild habitats.

Why are rainforests important?

Rainforests are home to billions of animals and plants. When rainforest trees are burned to clear the land for farming, they release carbon dioxide. That makes climate change worse.

Sun bear

What causes extinction?

Extinction is when a type of animal or plant dies out so there are none left on Earth. There are lots of reasons for extinction, but today humans are doing so much damage to the world that we are putting many animals at risk.

Going...
Beluga sturgeons are under threat because they are fished for their valuable eggs

Going...
Rhinos are hunted and killed because some people want their horns

Gone
Golden toads probably went extinct because of global warming

127

Where does all the rubbish go?

When we throw rubbish away we sort it into different bins. Some of it will end up in landfill or being burned, which is very bad for the environment. It's better to go zero! That means trying to create no rubbish at all.

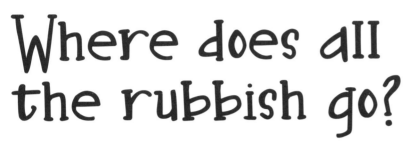

Painted turtles

Some of this rubbish will never rot. It will stay in the ground for hundreds, or even thousands of years.

What's that stink?

A landfill is a huge hole in the ground where rubbish is put. As the rubbish rots, it gives off methane. It's a more harmful greenhouse gas than carbon dioxide.

Grasshopper sparrow

Osprey

How can rubbish turn green?

Freshkills, in the USA, was once the world's biggest landfill. Now it's being turned into a park and more than 200 types of animal live there.

Why is rubbish a hot topic?

This rubbish is hot – burning hot! It's being burned in a big oven, called an incinerator. The rubbish is burned instead of being put into landfill. As it burns, it releases lots of pollution.

Five hundred steel cans can be recycled to build a bike!

How can I go zero?

If you recycle, or reuse, all your rubbish you have gone zero! Turn the page to discover how recycling and reusing helps to reduce the amount of rubbish that goes to landfill, or is burned.

What are the three Rs?

Reduce, Reuse and Recycle! By cutting down the amount of energy we use and waste we create, we can help to make Earth a better place.

REDUCE

Cutting down the amount of meat you eat can cut greenhouse gases.

REUSE

Using paper more than once means fewer trees will be cut down – and save a forest

RECYCLE

You can save energy by recycling. That helps protect Earth's atmosphere from damage.

Can poo be recycled?
Yes it can!

Elephant, rhino and kangaroo poo can be used to make paper

Llama poo can be burned on fires to keep people warm, or cook their food

The solid sludge that is collected at sewage farms can be turned into fertiliser. Farmers put it on their fields to help plants grow

How can we create less rubbish?

Plastic can be difficult to recycle, so try not to buy things that come in lots of plastic packaging.

Use a reusable water bottle and fill it with tap water.

Use a toothbrush made from bamboo, not plastic.

Carry your lunch in reusable tubs or beeswax wrappers instead of plastic wrap.

What are we doing to save the planet?

All over the world, people are working hard to save the planet for your future – at home, on farms and in the workplace. Saving the planet is a job for everyone.

What is conservation?
Conservation is the work people do to protect wild and special places.

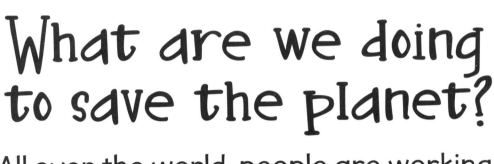

My job is to look after the Great Barrier Reef and teach people about the animals that live here.

We collect wood to burn at home, for cooking and heating, but we are planting new trees to replace the wood we use.

What's a solar farm?

A solar farm is a place with lots of solar panels. The panels collect sunlight and turn it into electricity.

The largest solar farms are in hot countries. They have more than 2 million solar panels.

I'm a solar-powered cleaning machine! At this solar farm in India, we keep the panels clear of sand so they can keep soaking up the sunlight.

I live in the Amazon rainforest. I take care of this precious habitat so it will still be here for my children and grandchildren.

I'm in Antarctica, counting penguins to see how healthy this colony is.

We can all do our part to help save the Earth!

A compendium of questions

How can I use less plastic?
Think about whether you need to buy a product in plastic. Liquid soap, for example, comes in plastic bottles, but a bar of soap is wrapped in paper.

How many tigers are in the wild?

There are only around 3900 tigers left in the world. Recently, conservation work has been able to stop their numbers from falling, but they still need our protection to live safely in the wild.

How can I feed wild birds?

The easiest way to feed wild birds is to grow lots of flowers that will make seeds for the birds to eat in winter. You can also buy bird food and hang it from trees in bird feeders.

It's a good idea to fill up a bird bath, or leave a bowl of water out so birds can drink and wash — far from any place where cats can hide!

What can I do for nature on a day out?

Enjoy looking at plants and animals, but avoid picking flowers or disturbing animal homes. Always take your rubbish home.

Flowers make bees happy!

What should I do with old clothes?

Clothes can be recycled, they can be cut up and used as rags for cleaning, or if they are in good condition you can sell or swap them, or take them to charity shops.

It's fun to make things, and now these cards won't be thrown away!

Can I make gifts instead of buying them?

Making gifts is a great way to reuse and recycle. You could turn old greetings cards into bookmarks and gift tags.

What's a swap-shop?

Instead of throwing things out, you can swap them! Set up a swap-shop where people can bring toys or books they have finished using, and trade them for something someone else has donated.

You could set up a swap-shop like this one at school.

What type of gift keeps on giving?

A plant! You can grow a tomato or bean plant from seed and give it to someone else.

What is a carbon footprint?

It is a measure of how much carbon dioxide is released into the atmosphere because of how you live you life. Cutting our carbon footprint will help in the battle against climate change.

How can I make an animal habitat?

Make a pile of logs, sticks and leaves in a shady place outside. Soon all sorts of bugs and small animals will be happy to make their home there.

index